A Women @ the Well Series

Just Thinking

About This - n - That

with Alexis & Me

C.L. LAWRENCE

Fallon House Publishing
Oaklyn, NJ

Copyright © 2018 by C.L. Lawrence

All rights reserved. No part of this publication may be reproduced, distributed or transmitted in any form or by any means, including photocopying, recording, or other electronic or mechanical methods, without the prior written permission of the publisher, except in the case of brief quotations embodied in critical reviews and certain other noncommercial uses permitted by copyright law. For permission requests, write to the publisher, addressed "Attention: Permissions Coordinator," at the address below.

C.L. Lawrence/Fallon House Publishers
P.O. Box 220
Oaklyn, NJ 08107
www.cllawrence.org

Ordering Information:
Quantity sales. Special discounts are available on quantity purchases by corporations, associations, and others. For details, contact the "Special Sales Department" at the address above.

Just Thinking About This-n-That w/Alexis & Me/ C.L. Lawrence —(Vol. 1) 1st ed.
ISBN 978-1946587008

Dedicated to

Mary Hamlett
(Medley Cousin-in-Law)

*My "Sista Girl" Friend
Thinker, Planner, Mover & Shaker*

Download your FREE eBook at CLLawrence.org & receive my blogcasts delivered to your email

DO YOU!
YOU ARE ANOINTED TO BE YOU
C.L. LAWRENCE

> Live as though you were to die tomorrow.
> Learn as though you were to live forever.
> — Mahatma Gandhi

Contents

INTRODUCTION
LITANY OF EMPOWERMENT

Chapter One
THE UNIQUE BLEND OF YOU   1

Chapter Two
ON CHOICE   11

Chapter Three
YOUR CIRCLE   29

Chapter Four
ON PURPOSE   45

Chapter Five
LIFESCAPING   53

Benediction
THINK ON THESE THINGS   61

INTRODUCTION

"We cannot solve our problems with the same level of thinking that created them."

— Albert Einstein

Just Thinking, *About This-n-That* w/Alexis & Me, is the first volume of spirit wisdom in the Women @ the Well Series; essays from conversations at the Well, morning talks with my amazing daughter, Alexis Fallon Medley, and chats with the writings of thinkers from 19th century thru today.

Now and then there's a quote, sermon, comment, notion, ideology, or a voice inside that begs to be given a second thought. Invite the wisdom of the Universe to join the conversation these thoughts stir inside. The result will be abundantly more than you could ask or think.

The Women @ the Well, Litany of Empowerment is ever evolving, because life is dynamic, and ever unfolding. As we rise to new echelons of thinking, deeper depths of understanding, new affirmations are needed, so always remain ready to receive.

In this little volume and those to follow, all that we receive we pour out. The Well is always open; you are welcome to drink.

Women @ The Well

With joy we draw water from the wells of salvation.
Isaiah 12:3

A Well gives access to the water that runs deep beneath the surface of the earth. To reach this life sustaining resource you must dig. Water, while symbolic of the Word of God, The Well offers the reflective imagery of gathering at the well drawing for the deep things of God, the sustenance of life that runs beneath the surface.

When women gather, we draw from the deeper place, from beneath the surface of things to find the life-giving truths to sustain us. When women gather @ The Well, we learn, share, teach give, and love,

When women gather, we give birth to ourselves as new creations; reproduce after our own kind in our daughters, granddaughters, all women in the earth; our sons, grandsons, and all men of the earth; in all who love life, desire to live in the Universe of Wisdom, wholeness and abundance. When women gather we draw water from the deep and pour out nourishing the earth.

At the Well are thinkers, seekers, faith walkers; women of decision, intelligence, discipline, purpose, & love.

Women @ The Well

Litany of Empowerment

I AM part of a sisterhood of unashamed women of Faith
I AM a thinker
I AM a learner
I AM a woman of Decision, Intelligence, Discipline, Purpose, & Love

I search diligently the Law of Love upon which my being is established; deep into the mine of my soul as one digs for gold and diamonds; and there find

Knowledge of my Power, Courage to Dare and Faith to Do

The die has been cast. I have stepped over the line onto the path of my divinely designed destiny.

The decision has been made. My past is redeemed. My present makes sense. My future is secure.

I AM finished with low living, sight walking, small planning, colorless dreaming, mundane talking, narrowmindedness, cloudy vision and dwarfed goals.

I AM fearfully and wonderfully made; goodness, mercy, forgiveness and prosperity are woven into the divine tapestry of my being.

I AM above the need for preeminence, position, promotions, plaudits, praise or popularity.

I AM above the need to be right, recognized, regarded or rewarded to know or affirm my worth and value.

I walk by faith, live on purpose, watch, control and alter my thoughts, run with patience, and labor by Spirit power.

My face is set. My focus fixed. My mission clear, to see God's purpose in me revealed.

Though my road, rough at times, mountains high, and valleys deep, I do not crumble to doubt and fear.

When life happens, and darkness looms, my guide, my comforter, my teacher is reliable.

I cannot be bought, lured, or tempted.

I cannot be discouraged, dissuaded, detoured, deluded or delayed because my mind is renewed, and

I AM transformed.

I give from my well, teach all I know, and work while it's day

I will not flinch in the face of sacrifice, cower in adversity, negotiate at the table of the enemy;

I will not ponder at the pool of popularity or meander in the maze of mediocrity because

I AM Decisive, Intelligent, Disciplined, Purposeful, Loving, and

(Oh, by the way)

I AM awesome.

Chapter One

THE UNIQUE BLEND OF YOU

Have you ever thought of yourself as a unique blend? You are. There's no one else like you, not even close. When someone says, "You remind me of _____." Or "You're just like _____." Of course, genetically there's family resemblance, or, perhaps subconsciously a mimicking of gestures or expressions of someone we've been around for a long time, but who we are goes deeper than that. There's infinitely more to you than what meets the eye.

You are a multifaceted, intricate composite of divinely selected characteristics[1] from the kaleidoscope of your DNA that goes back further than any online DNA or ancestry search could ever go. You're a composite of experiences, thoughts, interpretations, from your life's journey and the life journey of those who have poured into you that you've mixed and remixed in your own unique way. There's more to you than

---

[1] I praise you because I am fearfully and wonderfully made; your works are wonderful, I know that full well. Psalm 139:14

1

you think; more to you than what you see in the mirror or those around you.

Several people may have the same experience but differing feelings and draw dissimilar conclusions. There are gifts, talents, and skill sets, but within each is an array of operations. There are visualizations that only you possess. Dreams and ambitions that have been with you for a lifetime. You have no idea where they came from, but they're there.

There may be other dimensions, other facets of yourself inside that you struggle to be, or struggle to hide. Only you know. If you identify with the word struggle that means, there's a level of unrest and discomfort. Some live a lifetime of conformity to anesthetize the feelings of disappointment and unhappiness in not living in the fullness of who they are.

If someone were to ask you, "Who are you?" How would you answer the question? Would you answer stating your name? Someone might respond, "I'm Anna's daughter, Harold's son, Mary's cousin, or Jack's friend, defining themselves through their connection with someone else. Another may state their profession, "I'm a teacher" or "I'm an attorney," or "I'm a personal trainer," defining themselves by what they do. Stating your profession says what you do, and most likely what your skills and intellectual inclinations may be, but does it say who you are?

Can one really answer such a profound question so simply? Who you are is far too complex, evolving, and too interesting to capture in a sentence or do justice to yourself with so few words. No one thinks like you, feels like you, has your visions and passions. You are the unique blend of you. You are your own brand.

YOU ARE YOUR CHARACTER
YOUR CHARACTER IS YOU

Your character is the blossom, the totality of your thoughts about yourself and all matters of life. The culmination of everything you think about everything. The Bible helps with the question of who we are. Proverbs 23:7[2] is clear that the answer to who you are or any similar question, isn't your name, who your parents or associates are or what you do for a living. It says, the aggregate of what you think about *this and that* is who you are.

> As a man or woman thinks, so is he/she.
> Proverbs 23:7

Your character is the complete sum of your thoughts. Your thoughts are the fountain of your actions. Your character is the expression of everything you think about everything. The thoughts which you have built into your character have brought you to where you are at this juncture in your life, your present situation and even where you're standing at this precise moment. That's a challenging thought, think about it.

---

[2] As a man or woman thinks, so is he or she

Everything has a Because

Every effect has a cause. Everything that happens, happens because of something else that happened before that. You are who you are and where you are because of decisions you made before now that resulted in your now. You are the cause of your effect. That's a good thing because it means you can cause the effect you want in yourself and in your life in the future.

Everything comes from somewhere Nothing comes from nowhere

You are the sum of your thoughts in response to everything you've seen and heard around you since before you were conscious of thinking. Everything you heard about yourself or identified with became seeds planted in the soil of your soul. You are the harvest of the seeds planted all your life. You are the harvest of the hidden seeds of thoughts, ideas, philosophies, ideologies, religious orientation, mores . . . You are the harvest of the seeds of:

- What your mother and/or father said about you
- What you overheard someone say about you
- What your teachers said

- What your friends or bullies said
- What TV, billboards, magazine ads and society said about you and others like you

Every thought was a seed. Every word that proceeded from a thought was a seed. Seeds were planted, took root and being completely unaware, you nourished and cultivated the seeds with your thoughts and through the years with the memories. You acted upon a thought. Some you nurtured, some you didn't but the roots remain. Unless you consciously did something with them, they're still producing effect. You were driven to act on or ignore them, but they are "cause & effect."

Do you remember something unkind or demeaning someone said about you that pops up in your mind out of nowhere now and then? Whether a thoughtless comment or meant for evil, they said it and moved on, but it was the cause of an effect you've lived with.

Take a few minutes.

Think about it. **Identify** it. **Own/Disown** it. **Move** on.

_____
_____
_____
_____

Taking time to reflect and identify when and where bad seeds were planted can be uncomfortable, and maybe even painful – but you can do it. You've got what it takes. You have Knowledge of your Power, Courage to Dare and Faith to Do.[3]

By the way, if you think of something that <u>was</u> true, it may have happened to you, but ***it does not define you***. See it for what it was and move on.

YOU ARE WHO YOU DECIDE YOU ARE

That's challenging language, especially in a world that tells you who you are, what you ought to be, what your aspirations should be and what your limitations are. To think one has the power to define oneself and not receive whatever is thrown at them is intimidating. Perhaps, but, nevertheless, true. All that a person achieves or does not achieve is consistent with his/her own thoughts, habits and disciplines. That's the starting place, and there is no other.

The higher a person lifts their thoughts, the greater their success, the more lasting will be their achievements because a higher level of thinking attracts into one's orbit access to resources not available at a less lofty quality of mental habits.

---

[3] Women @ The Well Litany of Empowerment

A person can rise, win victories, and achieve by elevating their mental processes to the level of that which they want to attain. You want big, think big. You will not/cannot achieve big if your vision is small. You will never go after what you cannot see. You will not attain high with small goals. You don't need God, the Holy Spirit, the power of the Universe, the Wisdom of the Universal Mind for that which you can acquire on your own. Faith is not required for that which you can do for yourself.

The *faith walk*, the *step of faith*, the *stepping out on faith ideology* is believing, trusting God for what you can "see" (vision) but cannot attain in your own strength. If you have a vision for it, then it is possible. If it's big, even "too big," if you can see it, it's still possible. That's where the Universal Power steps in, to bring you and the impossible together. In this context, bringing you into the image/vision of yourself.

You rise to the level of your own expectation; not your wishes, hopes and fantasies, but your expectation and the demands that you put on yourself. Wishes require no action, nothing more than the breath it takes to make it. "Wish upon a star" makes nice poetry and song lyrics, but it has no power to do anything but give you a temporary *feel good* moment. Hope needs the participation of actions outside of yourself. Fantasies require only that you sit still and drift.

Being who you want to be, who you were created to be takes work, the ability to think, the courage to make wise choices and strong decisions in the interest of your highest good. You can only be good in the lives of others if you have built a strong and resolute you.

Stand in front of a full-length mirror.

Does what you see match the vision you have of yourself? Yes or No

If not, why not?

_____

_____

_____

_____

Rate your level of thinking: 1 – 10 (1 Low, 10 High)
               1 2 3 4 5 6 7 8 9 10

Are you satisfied with your rating? Yes or No
Explain:

If not, why not?

_____

_____

_____

_____

JUST THINKING ABOUT THIS-N-THAT | 9

Are you a big thinker? Yes or No

Do you have the courage to think big? Yes or No

Note and example:

_____

_____

_____

_____

_____

_____

Use this space to note what you think you need to do to bring yourself into the world of your vision.

_____

_____

_____

_____

_____

_____

_____

JUST THINKING ABOUT THIS-N-THAT | 10

Chapter Two

ON CHOICE

Have you ever asked yourself one of these questions?

- How did I get in this mess?
- What in the world happened that landed me here?
- What did I do to deserve this?
- What day was it I made the decision that got me on this road?

The short answer is, choices you made culminated into the reality in which you now exist. The result intentional/unintentional, every decision has a consequence, no matter the impetus, every cause an effect. Everything is a choice, every choice an effect.

You cannot live a choiceless life. Every day, every moment, every second, there is choice. While it's impossible to calculate with exactitude, according to researchers at Cornell University (Wansink and Sobal,

2007) estimates an adult makes about 35,000 remotely conscious decisions each day (in contrast a child makes about 3,000); 226.7 are food choices. As your level of responsibility increases, so does the smorgasbord of choices. We can choose what we will do with our life and the right to choose what we wish to experience:

- what to eat & eating habits
- what to wear
- what to purchase
- what we believe
- financial life (spend/save/invest/squander)
- giving habits
- in what city to live
- in what type of house to live
- with whom we spend our time
- who we date and marry
- have children/no children
- what we name our children
- what jobs/career choices we pursue
- how we vote
- what we say and how we say it

Consciously or subconsciously, we are what we have chosen to be. We are where we have chosen to be. We do what we choose to do. We have what we have chosen to have. The ability to choose is an incredible and exciting power with which we have been entrusted by God and for which we have an obligation to be good and wise stewards.

In our weakest state, we are still responsible for the governing, and accountable for the misgoverning of our bodies, finances, household, personal habits, professional ethics, ... It is ourselves and no one else who is responsible for the state of our lives at any point in time.

YOU ALWAYS HAVE A CHOICE

You may not like the choices you have. They may not be the easiest choices to make, but, know this, there is always a choice. Even to do nothing is a choice.

> To do nothing is a choice

You can look at any situation in your life and trace it back to the moment of choice. Like breadcrumbs, you can follow the trail that brought you to this point or put you in the situation you're in. It may have been a good choice, poor choice, informed or uninformed, conscious or subconscious, there was a choice made, and you made it. Even if you let someone else make the choice for you, that too was a choice. You either ascend to the divine perfection or you descend to the level of animal.

In the Biblical story, the Prodigal Son[4] perfectly illustrates Free Will, the freedom of choice, the power of choice, choice and consequences, choice and liability, (cause and effect) . . . .

---

[4] Luke 15:11-18

Note the choices he made:

- He chose to ask his father for his share of the family estate
- He chose to leave the safety, comfort and dignity of his father's house
- He chose to leave the covering of his father's good name
- He chose to live beneath his socio-economic status
- He chose the low-life lifestyle
- He chose to exchange his life of respect for riotous living
- He chose to squander his money instead of save, invest, & give
- He chose to consider eating what the pigs ate

He came to himself, a new level of thinking, hit the Reset button and exercised his power of choice. Notice the progression. "I will arise and go to my father, and will say unto him, Father, I have sinned against heaven, and before thee,"[5]

- He came to himself – He began to THINK differently
- I will arise – I choose to get up and take myself up from the low place of experience
- Go to my father – I choose to go back where I belong; to the blessedness I ignorantly and foolishly left
- I will say to him – He chooses the power of word
- I have sinned – He chooses to humble himself, formulate a confession and offer it.

---
[5] Luke 15:18

There is always a choice. Even if you get too far out from center, there is the choice to hit the Reset button and choose from a different standard or set of options. Whether you seek wise counsel (which is always good), whether you heed to the wise counsel you receive, at the end of all considerations, the choice is yours, and yours alone. You must live with the choices you make.

If you make a poor choice, a bad choice, or a downright stupid choice, which we've all done in the course of life, that isn't the signature of your fate. First, realize you're not alone. There are many in (or who have been in) the same boat. The defining moment of your life is the decision you make about what you'll do. Let me make it easy. Shake the dust, wash the dirt off,[6] seek the Universal Mind, Divine Intelligence, for the wisdom to correct, then keep it moving.

"Never give up. Never give up. Never give up."

"If you're going through hell, don't stop."

Sir Winston Churchill

---

[6] That he might sanctify and cleanse it with the washing of water by the word. Ephesians 5:26

CIRCUMSTANCE DOES NOT MAKE YOU CIRCUMSTANCE REVEALS YOU (TO YOURSELF)

You must have a good sense of who you are, who you think you are, and if you're not there yet, who you want to be. That's easier said than done. We know what's in us because we've been acquainted with ourselves since the day we looked at our hands and feet and realized they belonged to us. We know what's in us, but we don't know what we'll do with what's in us until we're tested. At the end of the trial, the test, the temptation, is when our character is revealed. Be careful not to be smug about anything because you may be surprised at yourself, surprised at your character. Pay close attention to yourself and don't take what you know about yourself lightly because the challenge to your character often comes unannounced.

Have a baseline, an individual foundation, a personal code of ethics, so you're not distracted by every shiny object that comes along. Consider this:

> [1] *When you sit to dine with a ruler,*
> *note well what is before you,*
> [2] *and put a knife to your throat*
> *if you are given to gluttony.*
> [3] *Do not crave his delicacies,*
> *for that food is deceptive.* – Proverbs 23:1-3

There's much packed into those few verses. Notice the caution about sitting at the table with a ruler, someone who has power over you. Gluttony is appetite, not just for food but for anything for which you're weak or crave. The verse suggests that the one who has power over you has what you want and if you're hungry, greedy, and undisciplined, you'll take what's in front of you, thoughtless of giving up your freedom, selling yourself into slavery. Think that's a little dramatic? Think again.

The second verse says, *"put a knife to your throat if you're given to gluttony."* Now, that's dramatic! Given to gluttony; you may as well end it all because you're as good as a dead man/woman if you're weak and powerless to your cravings and can't control your appetite (whatever it is). A dead man controls nothing.[7]

Let's be absolutely clear about the first thing. You do not have to accept every invitation that's extended. You know what you can handle. In compromising situations if you don't have a good sense of who you are and strength of character, you'll make a poor choice. <u>Choice means no one forces you</u>. You cannot blame. Yes, there are influences, triggers, emotional and otherwise, but ultimately all is before you on the buffet. The table is set. Consider a few of the choices:

- You choose to accept the invitation
- You choose to take a seat
- You choose to stay for the meal
- You choose what to eat

---

[7] DISCLAIMER: DON'T KILL YOURSELF - JUST GET A GRIP ON YOURSELF.

When you see clearly the circumstances before you, and look honestly at yourself and see the conflict with the Law upon which your being is established,

- Wisdom enters the room[8]
- Choices become clear as actual choices

You are where you are by the law which rules your being. Not chance, but the thoughts which you have built into your character have bought you to where you are.

Until you understand that you aren't a helpless victim of circumstances, but by your power of choice, you will always be banged around by the ebb and flow of external conditions and the choices of others. Whenever you abdicate your power to make a choice, someone else will make it for you.

There's no such thing as luck, good or bad. Opportunities and circumstances present themselves from the aggregate of decisions previously made and nurtured. A person descends into vice and low living by choices born of a mind cultivated in low life thoughts. A person ascends into virtuous living as a result of continued cultivation of good and right aspirations.

> You don't attract what you want, You attract what you are

In other words, if you got *low*, you chose low, nurtured the dynamics of low until finally it manifested into circumstances and conditions around you. If you have an upright life, worthy of honor, you chose that for yourself;

---

[8] or you hear the wisdom that speaks from within

applied the laws and principles that give birth to uprightness until it fit like a tailor-made garment.

Your life isn't governed by whims and fancies, hopes and maybes, but by your inmost thoughts nurtured by that upon which you choose to feed. You choose to shackle, or you choose to free yourself to be . . .

Do you know your appetites? Yes or No

How will you handle your power to choose in your future?

_____
_____
_____
_____
_____
_____
_____
_____

ABRACADABRA! PRESTO!! ALAKAZAM!!!

Magic? There is no magic, nor does the God of the Universe play favorites. If you want change, you must choose to change. People talk about the change they want and improving their circumstances, but most are unwilling to do much more than talk, talk, talk. Change requires sacrifice, crucifixion of self on some level. Well, that's an unpleasant thought, isn't it?

- If you want recognition in your profession, you must work smart (not hard). Read. Take courses. Get the next degree. Become the expert, the "go to" person. Be the one with the solution not the complaint. Learn. Give. Share your knowledge.

- Many diseases (not all, but many) are caused by overweight. Overweight is caused by poor eating habits, wrong foods and no exercise. Lose the weight so you can get off the pills. People stay on the medication, indulge their gluttony, and complain about the disease and the side effects of the medication.

- **THE LAW OF RECIPROCITY** is always at work. What goes around comes around. You reap what you sow. You get back what you give. Good or bad, or mediocre. True giving strikes at the level of sacrifice from time to time. Choose to go the extra mile to help someone with their project. Help someone else look good.

Finally, you cannot directly choose your circumstances, but you can choose the thoughts and decisions that will indirectly shape the circumstances.

CHOICE DICTATES YOUR REALITY

25 Choice Affirmations to help you shape your reality

1. I choose to be healthy
2. I choose to be wise
3. I choose to be repeatedly successful
4. I choose to be amazing
5. I choose to be courageous
6. I choose to be brave
7. I choose to be intrepid
8. I choose to be financially successful
9. I choose to be kind
10. I choose to be compassionate
11. I choose to be generous
12. I choose to be loving
13. I choose to have faith
14. I choose to believe in and act on my dreams
15. I choose to take bold actions
16. I choose to take the 1st step to achieve goals
17. I choose to believe I can
18. I choose to love myself unconditionally

19. I choose to love and accept myself fully
20. I choose to be kind to myself
21. I choose to attract wonderful opportunities
22. I choose good food for my body
23. I choose to have a regular workout routine
24. I choose to be a remarkable person
25. I choose to remain in a spirit of gratitude

This is just to get you started. Be confident enough to add your own "I choose" affirmations to the list.

Add at least five more affirmations to the list right now.

_____

_____

_____

_____

_____

_____

_____

_____

_____

_____

THERE IS NOTHING MORE POWERFUL THAN A DECISION

Apply the knowledge of your power[9] to make decisions that will result in being who you want to be.

God has graciously given men and women Free Will. That means we have the authority as masters of our fate and captains of our souls[10] to make decisions and the power to act on them. We have been given the right to choose the *highest good*, the *lesser good*, and the *no good* in every condition and circumstance of life. The God Mind within will speak to the God choice but you are free to make the God choice or the lesser choice.

A person with an objectionable character, who nurtures the low level, get over, "Slick Willy," loophole thinker, repeatedly decided to think that way until it became a subconscious paradigm. You are not Godly or righteous or good by chance. The good in you is a result of continued effort, habit, and disciplined practice, consciously or unconsciously, of right thinking, traveling the high road, choosing the better and best amid the varied grades of thoughts and attitudes.

We do not come to financial misfortune, poor credit scores, or threatening encounters with the legal system by the dictates of fate, but by undisciplined desires, rebellious and unteachable spirits. Even criminal behavior has its roots in felonious and unlawful thinking.

---

[9] Women @ the Well Litany of Power
[10] Invictus by William Ernest Henley

The good news is, you can be what you want to be just by changing the way you think. In Paul's letter to the Christians in Rome, he says, "be transformed by the renewing of your mind."[11] In other words, if you expect change, you must change the way you think before you can make a new decision for yourself. If you say, "I'm going to start healthy eating habits on January 1st or on your birthday next week, you've only made a declaration of your procrastination and questionable intent. There is no power required for that.

It's about making decisions that are in your best interest.[12] Is it that simple? Yes. A decision is a right now, in the moment, "real time," stake in the ground matter. The power is in the moment.

The moment of decision doesn't mean things will magically turn around. Magic is unreal and the illusion it creates is fleeting. The power in the moment of your decision, is the moment change begins to take place. That's the moment the Universe begins to move, and Spirit power begins to flow in the direction of your focus, bringing opportunities and people around you that will help facilitate the results for the decision you've made. It may take a while to manifest (maybe not), but one thing is certain, if you want something different, you must change the way you think.

---

[11] Romans 12:2b
[12] Women @ the Well Litany of Empowerment

In what ways do you need to change the way you think to be who you want to be?

_____

_____

_____

_____

_____

_____

In what ways do you need to change the way you think to bring about change in your circumstance?

_____

_____

_____

_____

_____

YOUR UNIQUE BLEND

Dreams are the seeds of the realities God planted in you before there ever was you (in the world). Your spirit knows and has seen the dreams, so dream big dreams, bigger than the ones you first imagined. You will become as small as the desire which controls you, or as great as that which you think most of being.

Cherish the visions and ideals that have been in your spirit since you were young. They were the promise and foreshadow of what God created you to be. Dance to the rhythm and melody that plays in your heart, appreciate the beauty that's in your mind, and the vibrant colors of your thoughts. That which you glorify in your mind and enthrone in your heart is what you will build your life by, and what you will become – the authenticity of what you were created to be, the unique blend of you.

NOTES

JUST THINKING ABOUT THIS-N-THAT | 28

Chapter Three

YOUR CIRCLE

The Bible tells a story about Achan,[13] an Israelite soldier in Joshua's army, who fought the battle of Jericho. God told the Israelites to destroy the entire city of Jericho because of its great sin. Usually the army that won the victory took the spoils (loot, pickings, leftovers), but God instructed them not to do that this time. Everything in Jericho was "cursed" or "devoted to destruction." God warned that anyone taking spoils from Jericho would "make the camp of Israel liable to destruction and bring trouble on it."[14] The Israelites obeyed, *except for Achan*, who stole a beautiful robe, gold and silver, and hid these things in his tent.

When his actions (disobedience, selfishness, deception, sneakiness, greed) were discovered,[15] God gave Achan a night to reconsider his sin and repent.[16] Achan choose not to do so.

---

[13] Joshua 7
[14] Joshua 6:18-19
[15] Numbers 32:23
[16] Joshua 7:13

His selfishness and greed were greater than his allegiance to God, family and community. Consequently, Achan, his entire family, and all his possessions were destroyed.

Consider this. Achan's sin, disobedience and poor character affected the entire nation of Israel. God said, "*the Israelites*" acted unfaithfully and that His anger burned "against Israel."[17] The nation, as a whole, was in a covenant (contract, agreement) relationship with God, so when one member broke the covenant (breached the contract), the entire nation's relationship with God was damaged. Achan's sin defiled the other members of the community as well as himself. He stole that which was "devoted to destruction" and brought destruction on himself and others.

> Who's in your camp?

Do you have someone around you who should not be there? Someone selfish, greedy, unjust in their dealings and has a rogue spirit. Someone with a negative, critical spirit, sneaky, and puts others down. Remember, their effects are infectious. They affect everyone around them to some degree, like a germ or virus. Don't gamble with your wellbeing by indulging the presence of someone in your life space whose poor character and bad habits WILL inevitably block the flow of your blessings. You must focus on God's presence and purposes in your life, your journey, your destiny.

---

[17] Joshua 7:1

WAKE-UP CALL

"We're the combined average of the five people with whom we spend the most time."
Jim Rohn, Personal Development Expert

NOW, PICK YOURSELF UP OFF THE FLOOR. That's a wake-up call. The people with whom you spend your time may be nice, sweet people in many ways, but they may not make up or compliment the picture you envision of yourself. You may have to use some photo editing software on the picture of your inner circle. You may need to airbrush someone out or overlay someone in.

You have the tools to create the picture of your life. No one else can do it for you. No one else can see the God vision you have in your soul for who and what you are; what you shall have; or what you shall be. They can see if you paint the picture for them, but you must first see it and own it for yourself. You will never be invested in what someone else sees or tells you is for you. God gives that to you first. When you own it, then you'll know who to bring into your inner circle. You'll know who fits. You'll know who belongs. You'll know the voices that create your harmony. If you want to fly, if you believe you can fly, you need to be around people who want to fly; people who've flown, who've seen life from a higher vantage point.

CHICKENS CAN'T FLY

The people around you significantly impact your progress. That which is around you rubs off. If you spend time with people who are:

- jealous
- critical
- unhappy
- grumpy
- complaining

you'll soon become the same. You need to be in the right mix. This may require you to prune off relationships that don't add positive energy to your life. If you hang around chickens, you'll never fly with eagles.

Don't spend your time with people who are:

- unmotivated
- sloppy habits
- going nowhere
- without goals and dreams

Don't spend your time with people who are:

- undisciplined
- have no focus
- lack integrity
- for whom mediocrity is the norm

They may not be bad people. They just aren't good for you!

You are full of gifts, talents and potential. You didn't earn it but it's your responsibility to protect yourself and to guard yourself and the treasures that reside within.

Who are the five people with whom you spend the most time and what do they contribute to your life? (Excluding spouse and children)

_____

_____

_____

_____

_____

_____

_____

_____

_____

_____

_____

_____

_____

_____

_____

YOUR INNER CIRCLE

In your inner circle are unequivocally the most important people in your purpose life.[18] This is the closest most valuable network of people in your world. Your Inner Circle is not your social circle, although there may be an overlap of one or two who reside in both. There may or may not be family members in your inner circle. These are they whom you reach out to first when you want to make certain your new idea makes sense. These are the ones you call when you have a mountain in front of you that needs to be moved. These are the friends whose advice you trust. These are the ones who can say, "That's a good idea, but tweak it or trash it," and you don't get offended.

> Your Inner Circle **is not** your Social Circle

Your inner circle are the people who are up close and personal, who know your hopes and dreams, your goals, and visions. They know your fears and weaknesses, want your highest good, want you to make it. Your inner circle are your champions, your mentors and coaches, your protectors, and at times the voice of your conscience. They celebrate your good and cover your bad. They find personal affirmation in your success. Your inner circle is bound by the Law of Love and the

---

[18] Excluding your spouse and children

Law of Reciprocity. There is mutual love and respect within the inner circle because you are to them what they are to you.

Create an Inner Circle Check List. Be intentional about a screening process. There's no set number but you don't need many. It's about quality, not quantity. You must guard yourself so before you allow anyone to get into your inner circle arena, vet them.

Who's in your inner circle? Why are they there? (Excluding spouse and children)

_____
_____
_____
_____
_____
_____
_____
_____
_____
_____
_____
_____

YOUR OUTER CIRCLE

With your outer circle you have less control over who's in and who's out. Your outer circle are people such as family, neighbors, or associates. That which differentiates your inner circle from your outer circle is the depth of friendship. There are those in your outer circle whom you may call "friend," but you can't share your deepest goals and visions. You know they won't understand. They may like you, applaud your efforts, but you can't bring them close. They may want the best for you, but they can't help you get there. Perhaps their world view is too small. Perhaps they have limited ability to see beyond where they are, or they don't have the faith that moves mountains. That's okay.

> Cherish who they are
> but let them
> stay where they are

BY INVITATION ONLY

How does one get the coveted privilege of being a part of your inner circle?

Good question. <u>You choose them</u>. Choose wisely those whom you invite to be in your close, personal space. Know that when you invite someone to be a part of your inner circle, you're inviting them into your life journey. You're judged by the company you keep. The people who are consistently around you, in many ways, define the perception of who you are and the heights to which you will go.

It isn't snobbish or condescending to hold the view that what a person brings to your life experience now and potentially, positions them to be considered a *candidate* for your inner circle. To think otherwise would be irresponsible. This is your life. You have only one and you're responsible to take care, nurture, develop, and protect it with wise decisions.

Enlarge your territory. Open yourself to relationships with people who have big ideas, big dreams, ambitious plans, meaningful purposes; people who generate the energy off which others can feed; energy that invigorates you to achieve your goals.

Be okay with someone God may bring into your world that may seem like an unlikely friend. The person may be of a different race, or socio-economic level. God will bring people into your life to whom you may never have reached out. God knows a lot of people, has a bigger network, and he knows who to send to impact your life for an amazing future.

Be intentional about having conversations with people who may think a little differently, not part of your religious affiliation, or family. Talk to people not in the same business, neighborhood, or workplace. The right people will come into your sphere Be ready to receive them.

THE JESUS MODEL

Let's consider the biblical model of inner circle/outer circle construct. Jesus got it right. He had thousands of followers, but he chose twelve to form his discipular[19] administrative structure. It wasn't whosoever came along could come along. He personally invited each one, carefully choosing the twelve, having the varied skills and expertise needed for the redemption plan. This clearly instructs that you must give vetting attention to who's in your inner circle and watchful of your outer circle as well.

Of the twelve there were only three men in his inner circle, Peter, James, John, and Mary Magdalene, who was always close by, but in the shadow of cultural mores. They were the ones with whom he shared his most personal thoughts, plans and ideas. They were the ones with whom he shared intimate moments of prayer, pain and disappointment.

What qualified them to be his inner circle? Surely there were many who were politicking for a spot in his inner circle, as there will be those who will lobby for a seat in yours. There isn't much said about this very important part of the Jesus story, but you can be certain, it was their personalities, character, strengths, love and devotion to him, and the roles they would play in the Jesus organization.

---

[19] Derived Form of disciple, discipular (dɪˈsɪpjʊlə) adjective

YOU WILL NEVER RISE ANY HIGHER THAN THE CIRCLE AROUND YOU

No one travels solo. Everyone has a host of visible and invisible people with them. All of whom come with the invitation. As much as possible you want to see who the invitee is bringing with them because ultimately, to a greater or lesser degree, their influence will be present. Words reveal the heart. Listen to their speech. People tell you exactly who they are.

The person(s) you're inviting may seem like a good fit, but as much as possible, you want to get a look at their inner circle to see who they're bringing with them. Your friend may have a friend that isn't your friend. Your friend may have associates you don't see. Though they're invisible to you, you may feel their presence and influence channeled through your friend. Influence via association is a fact you cannot control but you can be aware of it as much as possible. Come up with your own vetting criterion.

CONSIDER THESE CHARACTERISTICS

At the top of your list should be:

- Strong unshakeable faith
- Deeply rooted positive attitude
- Able to see great possibilities
- Strive to be their best self
- Wants others to be their best selves
- Likeminded people
- Believe in themselves (their abilities)
- Big thinkers
- Self-assured; Not given to jealousy or envy
- Big Vision
- Can celebrate others
- Able to think across generations
- Not greedy
- Open minded
- Respectful and non-judgmental

There's power in the spoken word. Death and life in the power of the tongue:

- People who speak life into your life;
- People who speak life, energy into the atmosphere
- People who speak positively about things and others
- People who send out praise for who God is, what he's done, and what he's capable of
- People who bless and encourage others

- People who have an Ephesians 3:20[20] faith?

These are just ideas to get your thinking started. Add your own criteria, that which is important in whom you have close to you. Use the space below to jot down a few thoughts on the subject in general.

_____
_____
_____
_____
_____
_____
_____
_____
_____
_____
_____

---

[20] Now to Him who is able to [carry out His purpose and] do superabundantly more than all that we dare ask or think [infinitely beyond our greatest prayers, hopes, or dreams], according to His power that is at work within us, Ephesians 3:20 Amplified Bible (AMP)

MY INNER CIRCLE VETTING CRITERIA

NOTES

Chapter Four

ON PURPOSE

When Eleanor walked into a room, everything got quiet; everyone stopped talking and looked at her. There was that freeze frame moment of silence and anticipation. What's she going to say? She was tall, thin, neither attractive or unattractive, but when she walked in, she owned the room. Sometimes she was only passing through and didn't connect with anyone, yet her presence demanded attention, even if only for a moment. What was it about her that said "pause" when you saw her coming? What was it about her that made you check for your own correctness if you were in a meeting with her? What was it about her that made you think twice before answering her question. She wasn't necessarily the one with the title, or authority, but she was undeniably the one with power and influence.

Eleanor walked with a purpose. Her whole aura had focus. Everything about her said:

- *I have a purpose for being here.*
- *I have prepared with excellence. Don't waste my time.*

Eleanor was organized, decisive and clearly thought driven. She was the "go to" person; the one to whom people looked for the nod or correction.

When you're clear about who you are and your purpose, you're comfortable in your own skin – you walk with a purpose. Those around you find for themselves a sense of comfort, confidence and situational well-being.

GOD HAS A PURPOSE FOR YOUR LIFE

You don't have to be religious, a church goer or have spent any time in Sunday School for this to make sense. God is **GOD!** God is big, created everything. God is Intelligence and intelligent. God is breathtakingly amazing. Beyond the comprehension of the created being, language, words, imagination, all inadequate to descriptively capture the awesomeness of the ultimate Divine Entity.

As far back as anyone can trace, God has been incredibly busy – yet took time to create you! Say it with me and repeat it until you ***get it***:

> "God took time to create me. With all the intricacies, complexities and demands of the universe, God took time to create me."

The point is, the conclusion from the feeblest understanding of God is this. God doesn't waste time; nor does God have time to waste. If God took time to create you, then the logical conclusion is, God had a purpose for doing so. I could rest my case here, but I won't.

An Old Testament prophet wrote: "I know the plans and thoughts that I have for you, says the Lord, thoughts and plans of peace, and not of evil, *to give you a future and* **an expected end.**"[21] Sounds like a plan. Sounds like purpose.

Created with plan and purpose means you are not coincidental and nothing is left to chance. All variables have been taken into consideration and provisions divinely put into place. All that which is necessary to manifest the divine purpose in you is available.[22] We have only to ask.[23] Ask with intelligence. God does not, nor is God obligated to supply in the present what you will need in the future. Eternity is in God's view, so our future is secure. If you don't have what you think you need, it's because you don't need it – yet! At the right time, in the right circumstance, in the right conditions, what you need will be right there.

The purpose and vision reside within the created being. It's our responsibility to discover purpose, live with purpose, and live on purpose. Without purpose, one lives life aimlessly. Aimlessness is trying this, that, and the other thing, or trying nothing.

---

[21] Jeremiah 29:11
[22] Philippians 4:19 But my God shall supply all your need according to his riches in glory by Christ Jesus
[23] James 4:2c ye have not, because ye ask not

AIMLESSNESS IS A VICE

Aimlessness is movement with no direction; movement without goal or purpose. Aimlessness is shooting willy nilly (all over the place) at no target or bullseye. Aimlessness is like lying on your back in the dark or daylight, shooting in the air and hoping to hit a pheasant. Aimlessness is waking up in the morning with no plan, just waiting to see what the day brings. Aimlessness is to have no yardstick for success or failure. Aimlessness is laziness. Aimlessness is complacency. Aimlessness is accidentally hitting any target or no target, and not caring either way. Aimlessness is never missing the mark because there is no mark to miss. Aimlessness is hitting something then trying to figure out what you hit and what to do with it.

Aimlessness is living in nothingness. A life of aimlessness is fertile ground for the roots of average to grow deep and mediocrity to become the norm. Aimlessness is ineffectiveness anywhere and everywhere.

If you allow yourself to be lulled into satisfaction with the complacency of ordinariness, and content with the usual, your spirit will become lethargic and numb. If you have no central, legitimate, meaningful purpose in your life outside of yourself, you sink into petty worries, complaining about things that don't matter, troubles that aren't your own, fears, self-pity, and that leads to failure, unhappiness and loss.

The writer of the letter to the Hebrews[24] said to lay aside the weight and the sin (vice) which does so easily distract, annoy and hamper our spiritual and personal growth, throwing us off our mark. The first thing to notice is the instruction to take action. To take action against something you must know what it is. The writer implies that you know what the distraction is.

> Declare war against Aimlessness and the Complacency of Ordinariness

To lay aside is to take deliberate, intentional, offensive action. The sin that besets will not go away on its own. Focus, *take it* (an assertive move), and lay it aside (an intentional move). Move the distraction out of your way. Don't take a passive approach and try to step over it or walk around it. Put away aimlessness.

WHAT IS YOUR PURPOSE?

What are you living for? What are you adding to the universe, to society, to the community? Breathing is

---

[24] Hebrews 12:1b Lay aside the weight and the sin (bad choices; poor judgement) that so easily trips us; causes us to stumble (fall off the wagon)

involuntary. If it were voluntary, what would be the purpose for which you would choose to breathe? You were born with gifts, talents, skills, . . . How are you using them to pour benefit into the lives of others?

Many people spend time trying to find happiness; their sweet spot in life, the "feel good." That's natural. Of course, it is a natural desire to be happy. The secret is, it's found in what you're able to give from that which was/is given to you. Who you are and what you have is a gift to humanity; a gift in the universe trying to find its place of egress. What you have, other's need. As you give, pour into the needs of others, others will pour into you.[25]

You must have a purpose and get about the business of accomplishing it. Devote yourself to it. Make it the center of your thoughts. If you think you have no great purpose, then do well, with excellence, that which has been given you to do, no matter how insignificant **you** think it may be.

Spend time with yourself regularly. Sit with yourself quietly. Listen to the thoughts that speak from your heart. Spirit in your heart will tell you of the purpose that lies within. Thought linked to purpose is a creative force. Set a goal, blinders secure and with laser focus, relentlessly pursue it.

You are a woman of Decision, Intelligence and Purpose, with Knowledge of your Power, Courage to Dare and Faith to Do.[26]

---

[25] The Law of Reciprocity. See "On Choice"
[26] Women @ the Well Litany of Empowerment

NOTES

JUST THINKING ABOUT THIS-N-THAT | 52

Chapter Five

LIFESCAPING

Think of your life as a garden. You have a garden even if you think you don't. There's something growing in the acreage of your life, be it a small backyard, a beautifully manicured, well planned landscape, an ill kept weeded patch of overgrown half brown dried up grass, or what looks like a waste land or landfill, it's your garden. Such as it is, it's yours, and the choice of what grows in your garden is yours. The landscape of your life is your **lifescape**, a reflection of the soil or garden of your mind.

What's in your garden? What seeds have you planted? Every thought is a seed. Every day you make decisions as to what it will look like and you care for it accordingly. You decide what will grow. You're the one who plants the seeds in YOUR garden. No one else. Not the people next door, the government, and certainly not the devil.

You have planted everything that has grown in your garden. Some seeds you remember; some you planted so long ago, you forgot you planted them. Some seeds you tossed aside unaware that your litter bug behavior was still an act of seed planting.

Thoughts, attitudes, habits, taken lightly or frivolously tossed aside, took root and now you see their fruit in your garden. Any seed allowed to fall into the garden of your mind, if not removed, will sooner or later blossom into action. Good thoughts, good fruit. Bad thoughts, bad fruit.

Seeds were planted in childhood before you were conscious of yourself as a being. As you grew there was the revelation of the hidden parts of your character. You're the one who cultivates your garden. You are the responsible gardener. Regardless of how or when seeds fell into the soil of your mind, you, the master gardener, must tend the garden of your mind, weeding out wrong and useless thoughts so that right and useful thoughts can grow.

Some plants take longer to bloom then others. Some take only weeks to show through the soil, like marigolds and tulips. Others take years like the Chinese Bamboo, that grows underground five years developing a massive root system before exponentially growing above ground the fifth year. Long time, short time, know this, you are the blossom today of the seeds planted in your yesterdays or yesteryears.

That's an Ah! Ha! an awakening thought. It explains a lot if you take time to think about it and reflect a little bit. Caution: Don't spend too much time in reflection. The purpose is not to arouse regret or guilt, but to affirm the truth that we are the manifestation of our past decisions, (and even prayers),

> Plant the seeds for the fruit you want to see.

malicious or well-intended, We are the reapers of our own harvest.

Wait! There's GOOD NEWS! Tomorrow your garden will show forth the seeds you plant today. If you want a different garden, a different lifescape, you must plant new and different seeds. You must plant the seeds of the fruit of which you want to see. New garden, new seeds. Plan the landscape you want to see, then tend it accordingly.

But what about the seeds already planted and roots already firmly in the ground of your soil? Good question. I'm glad you asked.

Plants, flowers, vines, of any kind will die if left unattended, without sunshine, water and fertilizer. Weeds will take over. You don't like the garden or any part of it; **STOP** tending it. **STOP** watering it with your tears. **STOP** fertilizing it with thoughts and memories. You can't un-plant those seeds. What's done is done. It is what it was. Just make up your mind you're going to **STOP** its growth. Besides, digging takes the time and energy you need to tend your new garden. Just **STOP** the

> **S – STARVE IT**
> Stop feeding it with your thoughts
>
> **T – THIRST IT**
> Stop watering it with your tears
>
> **O – OXYGEN OFF**
> Stop giving life giving breath.
> Stop talking about it
>
> **P – PREPARE NEW GROUND**
> Stop being lazy. Till your soil.

growth, let the old unwanted growth die from intentional malnutrition.

ANNUALS OR PERENNIALS

Get a new vision. See the garden (the life) you want and plant seeds that will bloom into the lifescape you want. This is your life so do your homework and plan the layout.

At the garden store there are two types of seeds, Annuals and Perennials. Annuals are temporary. They come up quickly, look pretty, but they have a short lifespan and you must dig them up and replant them each year. Because they only last through their season and need to be replanted isn't a reason not to plant them. They have purpose and aesthetic value of the landscape, adding color, fragrance and dimension.

> Anyone can redesign and replant their garden but not everyone will.

Perennials are planted only once and come up every year on their own. They tend to be less colorful, but they're the anchor plants. They give definition and overall shape, character, and distinctiveness to the landscape.

That's how people are in the garden of your life. Some are annuals, only there for a specific purpose and a specific time.

They aren't meant to stay forever. When their season is over, you must be courageous and remove them from your garden.

People in the other category are your perennials. Planted only once; they are your anchors; they don't come and go. Their roots are deep. They're meant to stay and if you care for them properly, they'll be with you through all seasons, year after year. They tend to be less colorful and flashy than the annuals, but their presence is strong and undeniable, adding to the uniqueness, character, and distinctiveness of your lifescape.

Plant the right new seeds and tend them. Give your attention to your new vision. Remember, you have Knowledge of your Power, Courage to Dare and Faith to Do.[27] Power flows in the direction of your attention.

It's hard work and it's expensive. Everything has a cost. Everything has a premium. You can't get something for nothing. You must pay the price for the new garden, the new lifescape. The cost is high: time, effort and discipline. You must tend the garden every day. The highest premium is on the faith that you can do it. Faith says, "Yes I can." With the Universal Mind in front, behind and within, redesign, replant, and tend your new garden.

---

[27] Women @ the Well Litany of Empowerment

What water have you drawn from The Well?

NOTES

JUST THINKING ABOUT THIS-N-THAT | 60

The Benediction

Finally, my brothers and sisters:
whatsoever things are *true,*
whatsoever things are *honest,*
whatsoever things are *just,*
whatsoever things are *pure,*
whatsoever things are *lovely,*
whatsoever things are of *good report;*
if there be any *virtue,*
if there be any *praise,*
think on these things.

Philippians 4:8

The Author

CL LAWRENCE, Thinker, Author, Pastor/Teacher, Leadership Development Strategist, Girlfriend, Mentor, Mom, & Spouse.

A dynamic Christian communicator best known for her eclectic approach and distinctive gift of discovering contemporary insights in the Biblical stories while maintaining the integrity of the text. She inspires you to think in new ways, take a fresh look at old assumptions that may be holding you back from making real that vision of your best self.

Her passion for excellence and outside the box thinking has made her a much sought-after conference speaker, trainer, and seminar facilitator. EXCITING. THOUGHT PROVOKING. EMPOWERING, are words used to describe her "Boot Camps," and other events.

She combines a 12-year tenure in Corporate America with 30+ years of pastoral and church leadership experience.

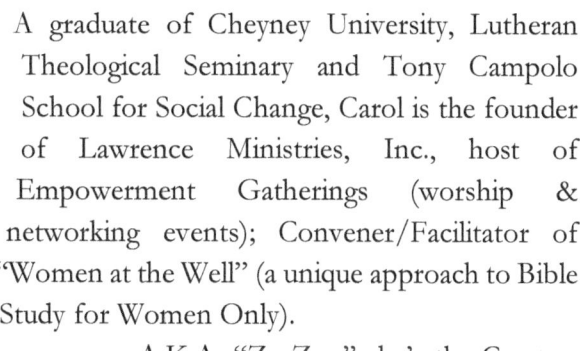

A graduate of Cheyney University, Lutheran Theological Seminary and Tony Campolo School for Social Change, Carol is the founder of Lawrence Ministries, Inc., host of Empowerment Gatherings (worship & networking events); Convener/Facilitator of "Women at the Well" (a unique approach to Bible Study for Women Only).

A.K.A. "ZseZse," she's the Creator, Host and Producer of the podcast "Jazz Divine; Zse-votions, (devotional CDs & MP3s); and the popular Blogcast, **"Just Thinking."**

To book an engagement
Email:
CL@CLLawrence.org
Visit
CLLawrence.org

Books You Need to Read to Prosper, Achieve & Succeed

Amazon.com
amazon.com/author/cllawrence

MOVING TO YOUR NEXT LEVEL
Walk, Don't Run

The Top 10 Secrets of Awfully Awesome People
Release the Awesome in you!

THE 10 COMMANDMENTS OF EXCELLENCE
For Preachers Only

www.ingramcontent.com/pod-product-compliance
Lightning Source LLC
Chambersburg PA
CBHW032211040426
42449CB00005B/546